THIS BOOK WAS WRITTEN BY

_____

_____

I KNOW YOU LOVES ME

BECAUSE

_____

I LOVE YOU BECAUSE

I LOVE IT WHEN YOU

YOU TAUGHT ME HOW TO

_____

I THINK YOU'RE NICE

AS

_____

WHEN I AM WITH YOU, WE LIKE TO

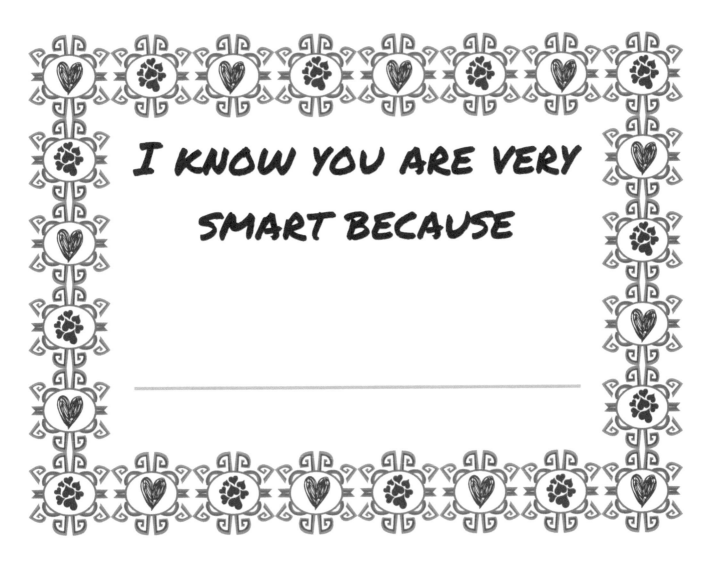

I KNOW YOU ARE VERY
SMART BECAUSE

YOU ARE GOOD AT

_____

YOU ARE SCARED OF

MY FAVORITE MEMORY WITH YOU

_____

YOU ALWAYS TELL ME

YOU ARE NOT GOOD AT

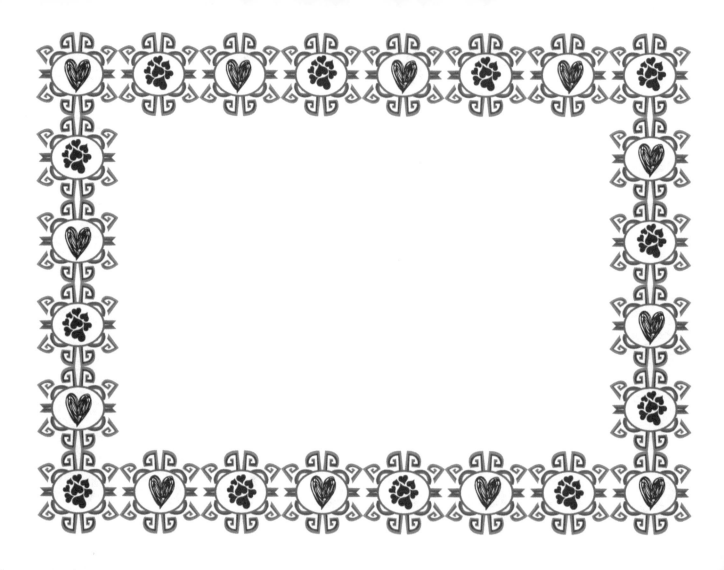

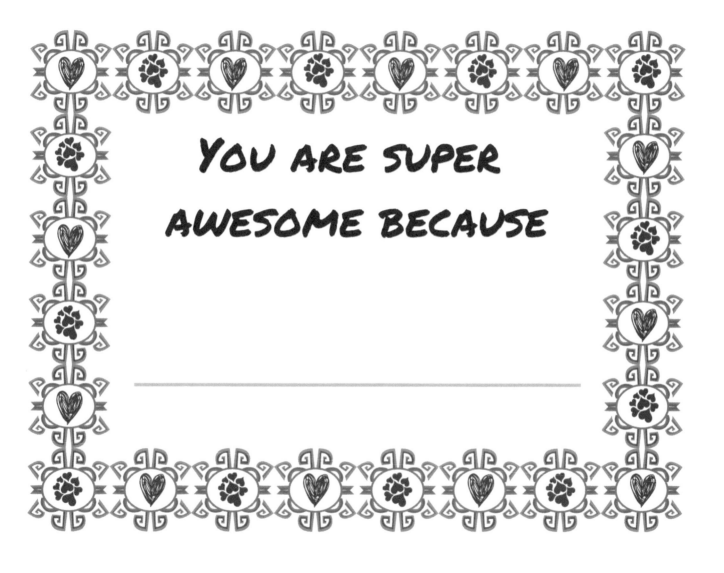

YOU ARE SUPER AWESOME BECAUSE

I WANT YOU TO KNOW THAT YOU ARE

_____

YOU ALWAYS MAKE ME HAPPY

YOU ALWAYS HELP

ME TO

_____

I LOVE IT WHEN YOU CALL ME

I LOVE IT WHEN YOU COOK

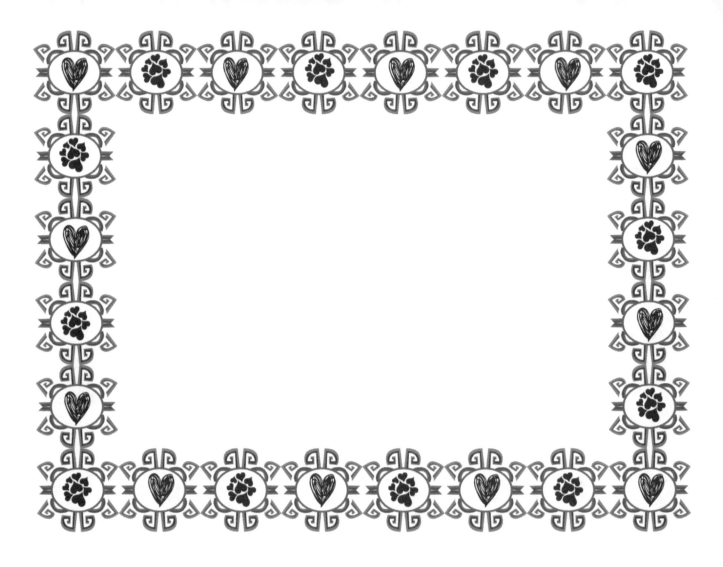

YOU LAUGH A LOT
WHEN I

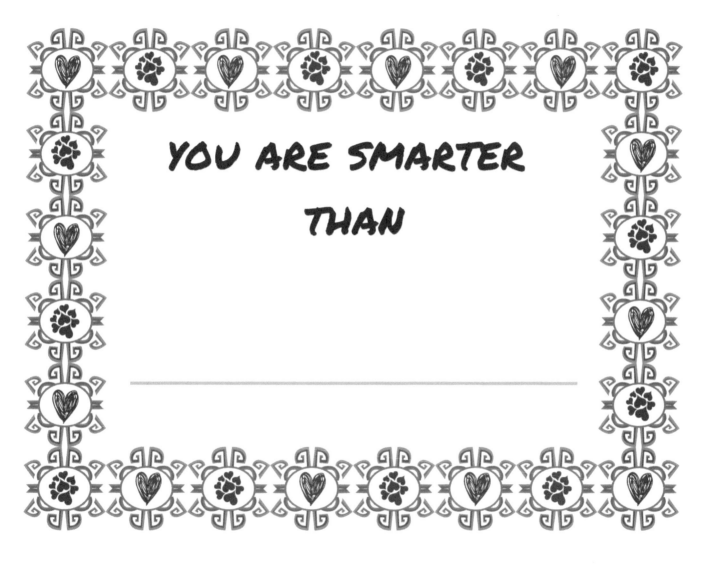

YOU ARE SMARTER

THAN

_____

MY FAVORITE THING ABOUT YOU IS

BEST THING ABOUT YOUR JOB IS

_____

WE LOVE TO DO
TOGETHER

YOUR FAVORITE FOOD IS

_____

I WISH I HAVE YOUR

_____

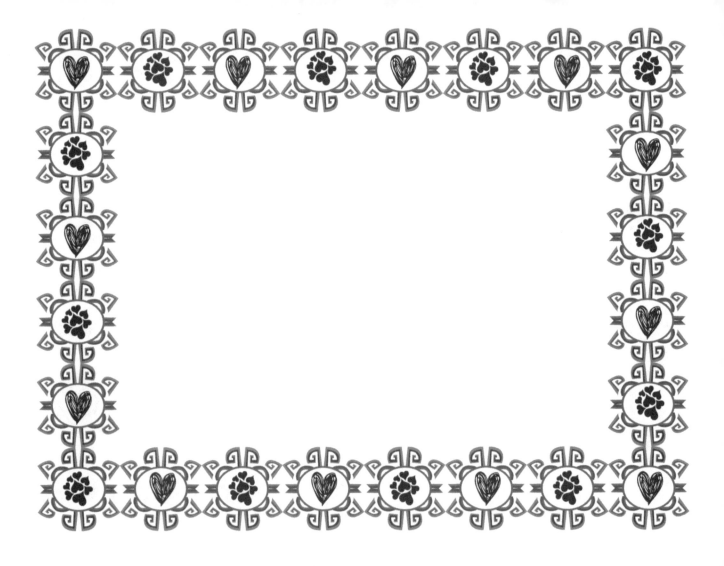

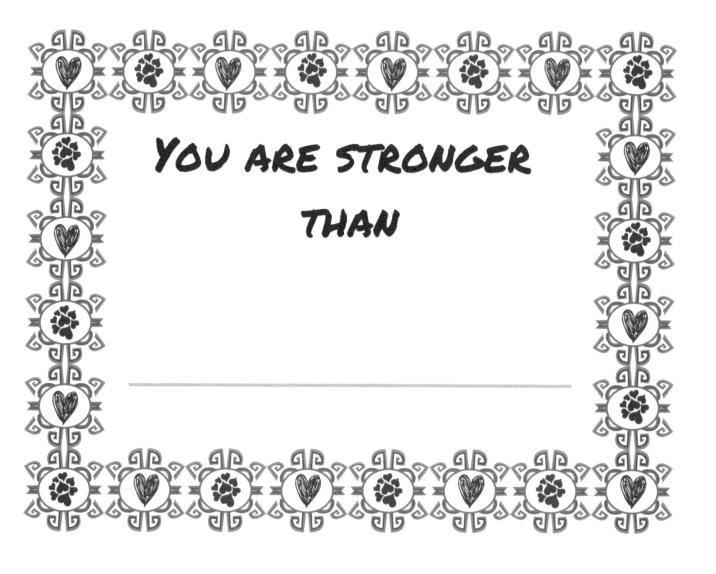

YOU ARE STRONGER

THAN

_____

YOU INSPIRE ME TO DO

_____

I ENJOYED A LOT WHEN WE WENT TO

_____

FUNNIEST THING YOU DO IS

_____

I FEEL SAFE WHEN YOU

_____

YOU DON'T CARE ABOUT

_____

I'M PROUD TO SAY YOU ARE

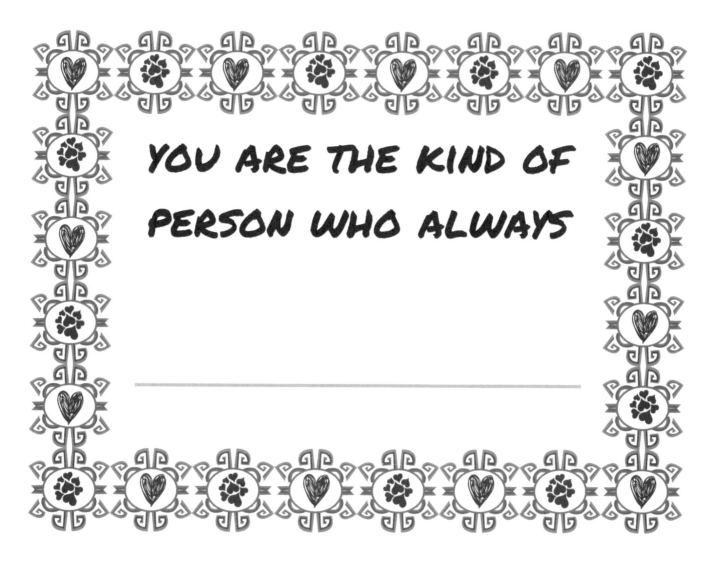

YOU ARE THE KIND OF PERSON WHO ALWAYS

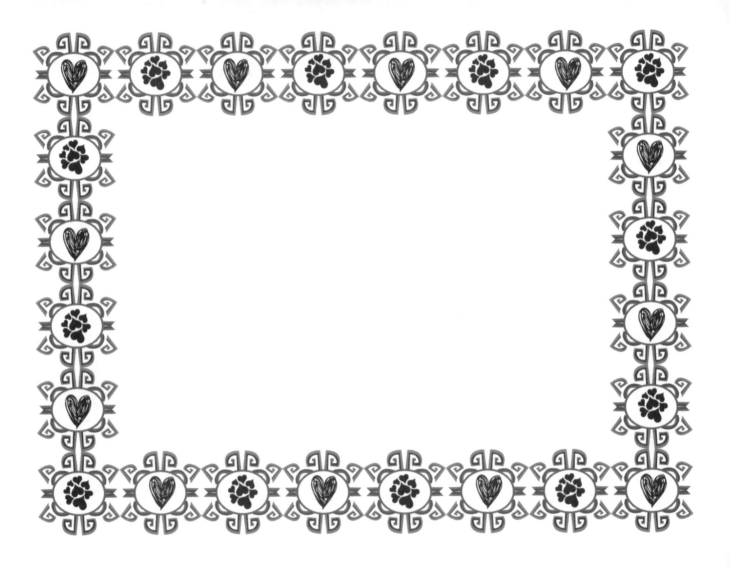

I HAVE NEVER SEEN
YOU

_____

YOU WILL ALWAYS

BE MY

_____

Made in United States
Troutdale, OR
12/21/2023